HACKING THE
INTERNSHIP
PROCESS

Part of the Work Book Series

By Zachary Schleien & Bill Hobbs

The La Plata Press

For More Information About

The Work Book Series

Books, Learning Materials, and Lectures
visit

www.theworkbookseries.com

"I was looking for internships on LinkedIn and got discouraged by seeing the number of applicants for every position. I couldn't see how I could stand out until I came across the hacking technique proposed by Zachary. The email hacking technique really helped to move my application forward."

— Anush P., Computer Science Student at Rutgers University, NJ

"As an international student this book has taught me how to reach out to recruiters, build relationships, and most importantly, helped me land my dream internship."

— Yip Tsui "Lucas", Information Management Student at Syracuse University

"We should all learn from Zach - not just what he does, but how he does it. He takes problems that we all deal with and finds creative and effective strategies to get results. This is the thinking we need more of."

— Joshua Kleyman, Former Advisor to the CTO of NYC

"As oversaturated and competitive as today's internship applicant population is, doing as much research as you can on the companies you are applying to is imperative. In my experience, making that extra effort to show initiative and interest is what has set me apart from the pack and gotten my foot in the door. This book highlights a series of hacks that help you effectively find and network with the necessary people at the companies you are targeting."

– John Gaebe, Marketing

"The job hunt process in the United States is very different to what I experienced back in India. The key thing here is networking, but being an introvert, I found it difficult to make genuine, professional connections. This is exactly where Rapportive's value comes into picture with special thanks to my friend Zach who introduced me to this hack. Prior to using Rapportive, I received only 4 calls out of 180 job applications. But by contacting the recruiter directly, I have received 8 interview calls so far from the total 30 jobs I applied to online."

– Bibhu Acharya, Information Management Student at
Syracuse University

Contents

FOREWORD
BY
BILL HOBBS

I've spent much of my professional life in the business world working across industries with leaders in Fortune 500's and founders in the Silicon Valley tech scene. There is a lot I have learned since my days as a student. A few years ago I wrote a book called *The WORK Book: How to Build Your Personal Brand and Get Hired.* The book has helped students understand the value of building and maintaining a strong personal brand. I wanted to get students thinking beyond their resumes. One way to do this is to participate in internships. Internships show employers that you have combined scholastic learning with practicable skills. That is, internships show, among other things, that you are able to take what you have learned in school and apply it to a profession.

After reading an article on Hacking the Internship process by this book's co-author Zach Schleien, I decided to team up with him, expand on the topic, and this book is the result of our efforts.

The goal of the book is to help guide you through the internship application process. We combine tactical approaches with technological tools and "hacks" so that you have the best chance of winning the internship of your dreams.

I had three internships throughout my college career, and the experience that I gained was foundational to discovering how business works in the real world. The internship experience, in turn, dramatically increased the value of my resume.

In addition to the demonstrating your capabilities, and developing job experience, internships help expand your network and increase your visibility in your chosen industry. This book is not a philosophical approach to what might work. Instead, this book is a tactical field guide to help you land your dream internship. We hope that you find the hacks useful as you work toward winning an internship and begin the journey towards a long and successful career.

INTRODUCTION:
WHAT THIS BOOK
WILL DO FOR YOU

As Bill explains in the forward, Hacking the Internship Process is a tactical guide to help you win an exceptional internship. Below is a brief explanation of what the book will deliver.

We give you the tools:

We will walk through how to land your ideal internship. We show you how to find the right internship for you, build a reliable network, connect with employers, prepare for interviews, and follow-up and close, all the while providing useful tips, hacks, templates, and real-life examples.

We help you plan:

This is a thorough process. We will provide you a methodology and structure to land an internship. We help you stay organized, and we provide tricks to keep you on task and stay focused.

We give you perspectives:

This book is a combination of ideas from two different perspectives, an employer and a recent student.

The employer's perspective is covered by Bill Hobbs, author of The WORK Book: How to Build Your Personal Brand and Get Hired! Bill has spent over a decade in the Fortune 500 world, interviewed hundreds of people, founded two successful companies, sold hundreds of millions of dollars in products and services across industries, and is currently a member of the board of advisors for several tech companies.

The student's perspective is covered by Zach

Schleien, blogger and recent graduate of Syracuse University's Masters of Science program in Information Management. Zach has recently navigated the internship process, hacked it, and helped his friends do the same. After a promising internship at a New York tech company, Zach used these techniques to land a full-time job with a Fortune 500 healthcare company.

Why this book?

The techniques described in this book are designed to help provide you with best possible tips and tools to secure your dream internship.

We have identified the most efficient and up to date technology to help you navigate and hack the internship process. Once you put in the work, finding your dream job later will be much easier. You can reuse these hacks after college and ease the pressure of finding the career that is right for you.

This book can be read from cover to cover as you work through the internship process. You may, however, decide to skip around from time to time, and that is perfectly fine with us.

A quick word on experience:

Many students worry that they don't have any noteworthy experience when the time comes for them to apply for internships. If you have no previous work experience, it isn't too late to start getting some. While you work through the process in this book, you can volunteer in the community, join a student organization, start a blog, join a startup on campus, join the school newspaper, attend a hackathon, or become a teaching assistant. You may even find a part-time job opening on campus. A little work experience will allow you to highlight some skills and experiences on your resume by the time you start applying for an internship. The goal is to illustrate your previous experiences and skills to your prospective employer.

Before we begin, below is a list of apps and resources that you will find useful as you complete the hacks in this book. Though the relevance of these tools may not be immediately apparent, you will want to check the appendix for a more in-depth explanation as they appear throughout the internship process. You may also want to download the apps and access the resources now so that you are more comfortable with them when the time comes for you to use them.

Download/Use/Investigate the following apps/tools/websites:

- iCal, Google Calendar, Outlook
- Google Inbox
- Notepad
- Rapportive
- Boomerang Respondable
- Yesware
- Evernote
- Glassdoor
- IFTTT
- Google Drive / Dropbox
- Trello
- Cold Turkey
- Grammarly
- Hemingway Editor
- About.me
- Somebody.io

CHAPTER ONE
RESEARCH JOB
DESCRIPTION HACK

Your goal for this hack is to develop a list of various job descriptions in several fields that interest you. Reading through a job description offers you a cache of great information. Job descriptions also offer many clues about the job and company, which can be found in the posting title, required skills section, and company description. Your list, once developed, will give you a sense of the types of internships that you will want to apply for. The list, however, should not be exclusionary. That is, if an internship opportunity that isn't on your list presents itself, you may still decide to apply anyway. But the idea is to be well-versed in the field you are looking to pursue. There is an added benefit in that your research will show when you begin interviewing for positions. When you are knowledgeable, you can ask more specific questions and people take you seriously.

Follow the steps below to develop a master list of job titles and descriptions.

Step 1: Write down all of the job titles that interest you. If none come to mind or you want to do further research, begin by searching for types of jobs applicable to your major. Aggregate plenty of job titles that pique your interest.

Step 2: Create a document called, "Job Descriptions."

Step 3: Search for each specific title using a career website such as LinkedIn or Indeed.

Step 4: Add at least 5 job descriptions/responsibilities to your document per job position. By looking at a variety of descriptions, you will develop a more complete understanding of that job.

Step 5: Read through the list and begin to discard positions that do not interest you. By the time you finish, you should have a master list of positions that you would consider applying for.

Step 6: Take notes, and write down questions as you read. You may also write down new and interesting information. Pay attention to keywords from the job descriptions that seem universal in each field that interests you. Jot these down too. You can reference these notes as you begin building your network, applying, and interviewing.

Step 7: Create a master copy of all job positions, their descriptions, and the keywords for each position.

Step 8: Write down the final list of job titles that interest you in a separate document.

When you are ready to begin applying for positions, you can use these job titles to find internship opportunities in each field. Be open throughout the process. If another internship position appears that interests you but is not on your original list, apply for it anyway.

Note: Before you begin to apply for internship positions in these fields, you should reach out to people who are in the positions at a senior level. This process is covered later in the "Could I be That Person in 5-7 Years?" hack. When you start reaching out to these contacts, your list will help you ask pointed questions so that you are sure that the position still interests you. Keep the list of positions and descriptions for later use. When you begin to apply to internships, you can use keywords that you found and add them to your cover letter and resume.

Key Takeaways:

- Research is an important part of preparation for anything you do, and finding an internship requires commitment to research and action.
- Your goal with this hack is to develop a strong list of various job descriptions in several fields that interest you.

CHAPTER TWO
HOW TO CRAFT YOUR ELEVATOR PITCH

Now that you have done your research, you can develop an elevator pitch that helps employers understand who you are. Imagine if you stepped into an elevator with a hiring manager, how would you describe yourself before the door opened and you both parted ways. That is the idea; an elevator pitch is a 30 second description of you and the value you could bring to a company.

The more tailored your message, the better chance you have to connect with the values of an employer. Many students have either no elevator pitch and wing it when they're asked to describe themselves, or they fall back to a generic elevator pitch. This is not good. If you wing it, you likely won't present a concise, organized, and effective pitch. A generic pitch, on the other hand, may be organized and concise but it likely won't grab the attention of an employer because it won't connect with the employer's specific values. A generic elevator pitch may include relevant information like the school you go to, your GPA, and major, but a tailored pitch will include these things plus specific information that connects your skills to the internship that you are seeking and the company you want to work for.

In the last chapter, we learned how to read a job description and identify clues about a company and the position. Research shows that most people listen effectively for less than 8 seconds[1] before determining whether to disengage. This means that a 30 second elevator pitch has to start strong in order to keep people interested throughout the entire 30 seconds.

You should also have a few variations of your "ask". The ask comes at the end of your elevator pitch and can be seen as your closer. That is, the ask portion of your pitch is designed to get your listener to either

[1]McSpadden, Kevin.

agree or disagree to something. We use "something" because you could be getting them to agree to hiring you, giving you an interview, referring you, etc. The stronger your pitch, the more likely you are to get you what you want. Here are some steps to building a great elevator pitch.

Begin with a salutation and handshake. You can open the conversation with a question to figure out the person's needs. The conversation might go like this:

"Hello, I'm Bill."

"Hi Bill. I'm Zach."

"Nice to meet you Zach. What brings you to the Big Data Meetup?"

"I am looking for interns for our tech team."

In this situation, I can tell him I'm looking for an internship and launch into my elevator pitch, but a better choice would be to uncover more information about what kind of interns he needs, what the interns will be doing, where they will be located, and other info that allows me to tailor my pitch to Zach's values.

"Oh that's great, Zach. What kind of internships are you looking to fill?"

"I'm looking for data analysts to help run modeling for a new product release."

"Oh, very cool! I have a friend who is looking for an internship in that field, would you like me to connect you?"

If the internship is not what you're looking for, you may be able to help them find someone who is interested. If you can help, then this is great. You will be able to expand your network and you may come back to the person you've helped at a later time for an internship or to help facilitate a connection. When you help people, they are more likely to return the favor later.

Let's say that Zach said, "I'm looking for interns for our summer retail management program."

I could then say, "Great, I'm looking for an internship in management as well." I could then launch into my elevator pitch or I could dig deeper for clues on what traits they need.

"That sounds exciting. How will you choose the right candidates from all these business administration majors?"

Zach can then tell me more about the criteria for the summer internship program before I jump into my pitch. He might say, "I'm looking for interns with great people skills, conflict resolution, and the desire to run one of our retail stores one day."

Now Zach has opened the door for me to pitch with some great info.

"That sounds very exciting! I'd be really interested in talking more with you about the summer program."

"Okay, great. Tell me about yourself, Bill."

"I am a sophomore business administration major with a marketing minor who loves **retail.** I worked in a retail landscaping store the last 3 summers. I really enjoy **helping customers and my team.** I won the employee of the month award several times for my high billings and ability to **quickly solve problems.** I would love to get into a program that teaches me to become a manager and develop a successful team."

I have now provided Zach with some valuable information including year, major, minor, (Purposely Omitted GPA), worked in retail (experience), I'm good with people, won awards for billings and conflict resolution (skills). I also showed interest in management and building a successful team. The one thing I'm lacking is "the ask" which I present at the end of my pitch:

"How can I join your team this summer as an intern, Zach?"

A question like this leaves no room for interpretation. Zach has very few options. He can either ask me in for an interview, ask to meet with me to learn more about me, offer to put me in touch with the person in charge, or flat out deny my ask.

It is unlikely that Zach will deny my request because of the work I did before delivering my pitch. However, if I had launched into my pitch too early without learning about his needs, I wouldn't have been able to deliver such a well-tailored pitch.

Your pitch should include your basic information:
Name
Major
GPA if excellent

And custom information tailored to your listeners needs:
Experience*
Skills*
Your interest in the field or opportunity*

Your ask*

The first set of information is the core of the pitch and won't change as much as the second set.

If Zach had said, "I'm looking for interns for our summer wholesale manager program," my pitch would need to speak to wholesale rather than retail. I might say this instead:

"I am a sophomore business administration major with a marketing minor who loves **business to business sales.** I've worked in a retail landscaping store the last 3 summers. I really enjoy helping customers and my team, but I learned a lot from our **wholesale partners about distribution and the value of an effective supply chain.** I won the employee of the month award several times for my high billings and ability to quickly solve problems, but I think having **strong relationships with our wholesale vendors** allowed me to get a lot of customer issues resolved quickly. I would love to get into a program that teaches me to become a **wholesale manager** and how to develop a successful team. I want to join your team, Zach. How can I make that happen?"

The core information stays the same, but the message is more catered to skills that speak specifically to the internship program I am applying for. All of this, or course, assumes that I really do want to work for Zach.

What you are doing when you are crafting a tailored elevator pitch is applying a highly effective rhetorical move called audience-based reasoning. Audience-based reasoning, as opposed to "me-based" reasoning, provides your listener with reasons that connect to his/her values and needs. Instead of using a "me- based" reason such as, I really would like to work for you because I need this internship for my future, you want to use reasons that your listener can readily connect to. Though it may be true that the internship is important for your future, this doesn't convince your listener that you are a good candidate. Put the listener's values first. This seems like a simple strategy, but we often revert to me-based reasons when we try to make a case that is important to us and in particular when we aren't fully prepared to make that case. Instead of convincing your listener/interviewer/etc. that you really need the internship (which really only matters to you), convince them that they really need you to intern for them. Listen first, so that you can determine what they are looking for in a candidate, and/or how they feel about their company. Then deliver your tailored pitch.

Remember, a tailored message allows both you and the employer to connect more effectively and should improve your chances to land the internship you want to get.

Key Takeaways:

- Curate the pitch to each employer.
- Your pitch should include basic information:
    Name
    Major
    GPA (if excellent)
- And tailored information:
    Experience
    Skills
    It should also include your interest in the field
        or opportunity.
    It should also include the "ask" last.

CHAPTER THREE
PROCRASTINATION HACK

In order to separate yourself from the other candidates searching for internships, you should maintain prompt and effective communication. No one likes to do all the research, communication, follow-up, and other work associated with landing an internship, but the candidates who embrace this process have a much greater chance at succeeding.

Let's face it; you are in college, and sticking to a schedule is something you have always planned to do... eventually. You schedule to work on your internship applications over the weekend. Your goal is to apply to 20 internships and email recruiters as well. However, when the weekend rolls around, the last thing you want to do is work on your internship applications, so you blow it off and promise you will do it sometime during the week. Of course, that doesn't happen and now you are stuck in a vicious cycle of procrastination.

You might be able to pull an all-nighter to squeak by on a paper or test, but all-nighters won't land you an internship. A minute wasted could be an opportunity lost in the internship world.

Fortunately for those of us prone to procrastination, technology and our increased understanding of the human mind now offer us some options. Here are a series of hacks to overcome your tendency to procrastinate and complete what is on your internship agenda.

Here are a few ways to get past procrastination:

1. Shower: When you begin to procrastinate, and find you would rather stay in your pajamas all day streaming media, jump into the shower. A nice shower can pull you out of a procrastination funk. Just don't shower all day!

2. Workout and/or Meditate: My favorite hack to get past procrastination and even prevent it from coming up is to workout. Another great way to get started is to meditate. Even if you aren't a seasoned meditator, taking a few moments to close your eyes and focus can help alleviate your stress level and kick-start your productivity.

3. Get out of your house: You may be tempted to hangout in your pajamas all day, but sometimes you need to get out of your house. Head to your local coffee shop (make sure it has WiFi) or stop by the library.

4. Create a to-do list: Add the most important tasks to the top of the list. When you see your "to do" list on your fridge and in big bold letters it says, "Finish Internship Apps", you know you have to finish those internship applications. You don't necessarily have to do the first thing on your list, but you should do something on the list. Sometimes thinking about the number of things you have to do is daunting. But organizing them into a list allows you to focus on tasks one at a time. Lists can alleviate your stress level and give you a

sense of completion each time you check off a task.

5. Don't go out the night before: That may not be an option for some of you, but if you are truly committed to this process, you will have to make some sacrifices. Get a good night's rest and skip the alcohol for an evening. When you wake up, you will feel refreshed and ready to take on your internship applications.

6. Block your favorite websites: Use the Cold Turkey app (see Appendix) if you can't stop streaming shows and going on social media every 5 minutes. You can Blacklist the sites that are distracting you from getting your internship applications complete.

7. Just start: I know that seems simple, but often when you get started, you realize the work that you have been fretting over is actually not too bad.

Lastly, a word on IFTTT

When you work on getting an internship, you must take steps to mitigate interruptions. Below are a few tools to empower you to automate tasks, stay focused, and of course, stop procrastinating.

IFTTT helps automate your life by creating connections between apps such as Facebook, Google Calendar, Twitter, and Gmail. Each of these automations are called "Recipes". You can install IFTTT on your smartphone.

1. Do Not Disturb: With just the push of a button, the IFTTT app can block off an hour in your Google Calendar as "Do Not Disturb".

https://ifttt.com/recipes/192149-block-off-the-next-hour-as-do-not-disturb

2. Get an SMS alert before any event starts on your Google Calendar: If you have trouble being on time, this recipe is for you. You can get an alert before your phone interview or in-person meeting, so you never have to make an excuse for being late.

https://ifttt.com/recipes/13-get-an-sms-alert-before-any-event-starts-on-your-google-calendar

3. Text yourself a reminder every day to not procrastinate: Sometimes you need an external source to get

you motivated. With IFTTT you can use this Recipe to send yourself a text reminder to get to work.

Key Takeaways:

- Block out distractions when you have set time aside to work on the internship search.
- Create a to do list, adding the most important tasks to the top of the list.
- Follow your list!

CHAPTER FOUR
BUILDING A REFERRAL STRATEGY

In sales, a referral is the easiest type of business to close because a buyer recommends the seller to other buyers. These types of business relationships are built on trust. In the job market, similar principles apply to landing an internship. If someone recommends a candidate to a hiring manager, the manager is much more likely to meet and interview the candidate. Hiring managers may even take referral meetings even if they don't have a position open and then refer you to someone in their field who does. This is why it is important to have a strong referral network to rely on when you begin applying for internships. In this section, we walk you through how to develop a strategy to build a referral network.

Before you begin your internship search, make a list of who you know that can recommend you to an employer. If you have a friend who works at a company you are interested in interning for, add them to your referral list. Outside of friends and family, you may not have a large referral network, so you should try to identify "bridges" within the network you already have. A bridge is a person who can connect you to vast networks of people and make building your referral network much easier. Bridges may not be the people who interview you; however, through their connections you can meet plenty of people who will. You should also try to find bridges within the networks you are introduced to in order to create a chain of new interview opportunities.

Ties: Strong and Weak

You can think of the relationships you have with people as strong or weak ties. You can think of strong ties as your friends and weak ties as your acquaintances, as described by Mark Granovetter, a sociologist and professor at Stanford University. Weak ties are critical to connect groups of strong ties together, and they can lead you to new relationships and referrals.[2]

In order to build your referral strategy, follow the steps below:

Step 1: Write down a list of your strong ties and the companies where they work.

Step 2: Write down a list of your weak ties and the companies where they work.

Step 3: Personally ask your strong ties for a referral to someone in the industry where you'd like to intern.

Step 4: When asking for introductions on LinkedIn (described in a later chapter), check to see if you have any first connections. If you have first connections, reach out to your weak ties by asking for an introduction.

[2] Granovetter, Mark. p. 205

The following are some weak tie examples to help you get started:

- Alumni in your fraternity or sorority
- Professors
- LinkedIn connections
- Facebook friends
- Your parents' or family's friends

If you would like to learn more about network theory and social behavior, I recommend Malcolm Gladwell's book *The Tipping Point* and David Easley and Jon Kleinberg's book *Networks, Crowds, and Markets: Reasoning about a Highly Connected World.*

As you build your network through your weak and strong ties, continuously add to your referral list. As an added bonus, indicate who referred you to who. This will keep you organized when crafting emails to your referrals.

Key Takeaways:
- Before you begin your internship search, make a list of possible referrals.

- You can think of the relationships you have with people as strong or weak ties. Weak ties are your acquaintances. Strong ties are your friends and family, people you have worked with in the past, and professors with whom you've built a good rapport. Weak ties are critical in connecting groups of strong ties together and lead you to new relationships and referrals.

CHAPTER FIVE
LEVERAGING YOUR UNIVERSITY NETWORK

Your university or college can be a great source of networking. Career Services and Faculty Advisors can be helpful with identifying internship opportunities through partner companies that are available in their employer network. They can also be a great resource to connect you with alumni that now work in your field of interest. The earlier you engage career services and faculty advisors, the better your odds are for success.

LinkedIn alumni groups are another great way to connect with alumni and help you find referrals and trusted partners in your search to land your dream internship. When I was hacking my internship, I received three responses over LinkedIn and two additional direct emails in less than 24 hours because of my LinkedIn alumni group. If you are in the early stages of exploring internships, then your main concern is to continue building a referral network. With that being said, if an opportunity for an internship presents itself, then you can certainly pursue it. As always, be direct with these individuals that are offering a hand (remember people are more willing to help when you are specific). It may take a couple of conversations before your alumni connect you to someone they know is hiring, but nevertheless, these contacts are vital.

Here are the steps to utilize LinkedIn alumni groups:

Step 1: Find your University LinkedIn group.

Step 2: Write your major and what you are looking for in the conversation title.

Step 3: Introduce yourself in the detail box.

Here is an example to help you fashion your own introduction:

Subject: Marketing Major Seeking Advice and Opportunities

Hi everyone! I'm in my junior year at (Your College/University) and I am looking for internship opportunities in the (your area of interest). If you're available, I would love to meet you for a cup of coffee or chat over the phone. Please direct message me or shoot me an email at (your email) Thanks!

I kept up with the alumni contacts I made throughout the internship process and afterward. They were willing to help me expand my network and even threw a few helpful tips my way. Even if someone can't immediately help you out, the connections you make by leveraging your university network can pay off down the road (particularly if they work in a company you'd be interested in interning for).

Key Takeaways:

- Your University or College can be a great resource to connect you with alumni who now work in your field of interest. The earlier you engage career services and faculty advisors, the better your odds are for success.

- LinkedIn alumni groups are another great way to connect with alumni and help you find referrals and trusted partners in your search to land your dream internship.

CHAPTER SIX
LINKEDIN
HACK

In this chapter, I provide you with a tool that you will use specifically for the, "Could I be that Person in 5-7 Years Hack?" and the "Search Companies Hack." Here you will get the steps to reach out to new people, introduce yourself, and depending on your progress through the internship process, either add them to your referral network or ask them about an internship opportunity. For this chapter, just focus on the steps to hack LinkedIn. You may want to return to this chapter to follow these steps when the other hacks direct you to do so.

CAUTION: The techniques below are designed to help you identify the e-mail addresses of the appropriate contacts for your employment search. You should not use these techniques to "blast" e-mails to multiple persons, which could be considered "spam" – unsolicited electronic mail advertising. Thirty-seven states and the federal government have anti-spam laws. The majority of these state laws target commercial or fraudulent electronic mail; a smaller number of state laws apply to unsolicited "bulk" e-mail.

1. Download Rapportive plug-in for Gmail

If you haven't done so already, download the tool, Rapportive. You will use Rapportive to reverse engineer email addresses. By reverse engineer emails, I mean that you will be able to figure out the email addresses of people you have never had contact with before. Rapportive will reveal whether the email address you have entered into the address bar is an actual email address or not. Add Rapportive to Gmail at rapportive. com.

2. Search for your contact using LinkedIn

If you are building your referral network, then you can use LinkedIn's search function to find contacts in your field of interest. You may start by searching a company you like and then narrow your results according to the positions of the employees. Or you may start by searching a specific job title that interests you and then narrow the results by company.

Later in the internship process, you will use this same strategy to contact prospective employers. For example, if you had applied to the company LIFT Protein Muffins for example. You would search LIFT Protein Muffins and then narrow the results into your "future boss" (the person who you would intern for) and recruiters at the company.

3. Utilizing Filters

Once you apply the search, use the LinkedIn filters to help narrow down your results. You can filter by "Company," "Industry," "Function," and many others. You may decide to start by filtering by "University" because alumni are typically pretty responsive. Another great filter is "Experience Level" or "Years of Experience." The rule of thumb is to target people in a senior position, since they have experience and influence over others who just started their career. You can also filter by "Location." Make sure to reach out to people who are in the area where you would like to live. In other words, if you are applying for positions in New York, don't reach out to senior management in London by mistake.

4. Find the URL of the company

Once you have identified your target on LinkedIn (regardless of where you are in the internship the process), find the URL of the company. The person's email will most likely end with the company website. You can do a quick web search to find the company's URL if you are unsure of exactly what it is. For the example below, I have used a made up recruiter who works at LIFT Protein Muffins named, Bill Smith.

5. Try different email combinations

Copy and paste your contact's name and company URL into your Gmail where it says "To." You can start with the first name, last name, @, URL (exclude "http//:" and "www." from the URL, and make sure there are no spaces). So, the first email you would try with Bill Smith would be billsmith@liftproteinmuffins. com. When you hover your mouse over the email address, the Rapportive app will tell you whether the address exists or not. If your first combination does not work, try others. You can add all of the potential emails to the "To:" column at the same time.

You will know you have successfully reverse engineered the employee's email when the employee's picture appears on the right hand side of your Gmail thanks to the Rapportive plugin.

In the picture below I have used my personal email address. When I type in my email, zachschleien@ gmail.com, into the "To" section of Gmail, Rapportive displays my name and image. This means that zachschleien@gmail.com is indeed a real email address.

6. Possible email combinations to test

Let's go back to our made up employee, Bill Smith, from LIFT Protein Muffins. I recommend trying the combinations below. I have found that first name dot last name @ the URL of the company is the most common email address. Possible email combinations may include:

billsmith@liftproteinmuffins.com (Most common)
bill.smith@liftproteinmuffins.com (Most common)
bsmith@liftproteinmuffins.com
bs@liftproteinmuffins.com
smith@liftproteinmuffins.com
bill@liftproteinmuffins.com
Bill Smith's twitter handle @liftproteinmuffins.com

If you try all of these combinations and none of them hit, you will have to move on to another person or another company.

7. Once you reverse engineer the email

Once you nail it do the Cha-cha-cha, give a fist pump, and pray that the individual will get back to you.

Tip: Make sure not to overdo it (spam employers). Limit your emails to one person per company every 3-5 days. People will find it obnoxious if you email the whole department. If a person does not respond to your email after a few days, try someone else from the company.

Below is a sample email you can model after when applying to internships (see the "Could I be that Person in 5 -7 Years Hack?" for a sample email to reach out for a connection). When you cold email recruiters you can use a summary of your cover letter.

(Employee's first or last name,)

I'm an avid user of (the company name). I applied for the (internship) position. I came across you on LinkedIn and was very interested in your expertise. I'm a junior in the (Your Program/Major) at (Your College/University). My passion lies in (your passions). During college (state an appropriate achievement and describe what you did).

This summer my goals are to contribute to a (the company industry) and to be part of a strong learning environment. Given my experience, I know I can be a valuable asset to your company. I know you are busy, but if you have some time to chat over the phone or grab a coffee, I would really appreciate it. I can be contacted at (your email) and reached at (your telephone number). My resume is attached.

Best,
(your name)

Tip: If you are not an avid user of the contact's service, say something that caught your eye about his or her company, whether that is a news item, achievement, or something about the company that you appreciate. You might want to apply Yesware's email tracking tool and edit your email with Boomerang Respondable before you click send.

8. Record your progress

It is extremely important to stay organized during the internship process, so make a list of your emails. List the company name, the employee's name, title, email, and the date you emailed them, so you can email someone else from the company if they don't respond within 3-5 days. If you do end up emailing someone else from the company, the likelihood is that they use the same email format, so there is less guesswork the second time around. Place this table in a folder you can find easily.

Here is a mock example below:

Company Name	Employee Name	Title	Email	Date Emailed
LIFT Protein Muffins	Zachary Schleien	Head of Marketing	zachary@liftproteinmuffins.com	10/4/16
The WORK Book	Bill Hobbs	Head of Sales	bill.hobbs@theworkbook.com	10/4/16
My Tiny Wins	John Doe	Business Analyst	john.doe@mytinywins.com	10/5/16
Crony Paleo	Michelle Smith	Marketing Analytics	msmith@cronypaleo.com	10/5/16

Key Takeaways:

- Download the Rapportive plugin for Gmail.
- Utilize LinkedIn filters.
- Find the URL of the company when you begin to send emails.
- Try different email combinations to reverse engineer an employer's email.
- Send a cold email that is well thought out.
- Record your progress.
- Follow your call or in-person interview with a thank you email the next day.

CHAPTER SEVEN
RESEARCHING CONTACTS HACK

In this chapter, we show you how to create a research document for expanding your network and/or preparing for a phone or In-person interview. The more detail you have about your contacts (things like, their work history, accomplishments, and motivations), the easier it will be for you connect with them during an interview or meeting. In this section we show you how to create an extensive research guide. These guides are particularly helpful when it is time for you to interview. An abbreviated research guide (such as the one in the example that follows the list) will help you with your "5-7 Years" conversations.

The following shows you how to make a Master Research Guide in eight simple steps:

1. Create a document.

2. Add the contact's/interviewer's photo to the top of the document with his or her name and position. A photo allows you visualize the person beforehand. Even if you are only speaking over the phone, it will help humanize the interaction.

3. Review the contact's/interviewer's LinkedIn, and add all of his or her pertinent credentials with a brief description next to each.

4. Review the contact's/interviewer's twitter. Read the articles that he or she has shared. You can address these articles in your conversation as they relate.

5. Review his or her podcasts (if available). Before one of my interviews, I listened to two podcasts that my contact was on. As a result, I was able to strengthen our connection by connecting a few points I made

to some things she said on her podcast.

6. Make a hypothesis. Brainstorm what is important to your contact. For example, if you are interviewing for a data analyst role, the contact may be passionate about something like decreasing churn at his or her SaaS company, so speak to that. You may want to brief yourself on the topics that interest your inter-viewer/contact so you can increase your opportuni-ties to connect.

7. Add your experiences. After you have learned ev-erything about your contact/interviewer, add your own experiences that relate. Also, jot down a few experiences that you think will come up during the interview. For example, if you are going for a sales position, you can share your experiences where you met your sales goals or where you had a failure and learned from the experience.

8. Practice: Review your document prior to your in-terview. If it is an in-person interview, do not show your document to your interviewer. Instead, prac-

tice before you arrive. If it is a telephone interview, feel free to leave the document next to you and use it as a sort of cheat sheet.

Sample Research/Call Template for the "Could I be that Person in 5-7 Years?" (Keep in mind that the guide you create for your internship interviews will be much more detailed):

First add the contact's photo and name. Pull relevant info from his or her LinkedIn. Write "the intention of the call is to hear from your contact" so you remember that the call is not for you to try to impress the contact, but rather, to learn about the contact and his/her field. Add a step by step script in case you freeze up.

Make sure to do your research beforehand. Your contacts will notice when you are in mid-conversation and ask them about their previous jobs or reference something they've done. These simple, yet overlooked hacks could make your new contact into your champion (someone who will offer you an internship or someone who will introduce you to the people in his or her network).

Bill: Call Template

Director of Digital Marketing at The Work Book

First, I will thank Bill.

Share with Bill that I am an undergraduate student at Syracuse University in the Marketing Program.

I am the marketing coordinator for a student organization at Syracuse University.

I currently run a blog where I am responsible for the Google Analytics, marketing, and develop strategic partnerships.

I program in HTML, CSS, and R.

Questions to ask Bill:

What do you do on a day-to-day basis?

What are the biggest challenges you've faced?

Do you do digital marketing as well as outreach?

What is your favorite thing about your current position?

What do you now know that you wish you knew starting out?

About Bill:

Bill's Specialties: Email Marketing, Analytics, Facebook Marketing, Google Analytics, Adwords, Social Media Marketing, Facebook Apps, A/B testing

With twelve years of experience with emerging technologies and startups

Bill was the Senior Account Manager at The Work Book for 3 years. In that role, he built, maintained and analyzed data sets to suggest how clients could improve post reach and visibility for their brands.

Because of the organic nature of conversation, you may not follow your template chronologically. You may not even get to all of the information. View your template as a source of information to prepare you to ask intelligent questions that show you have done your research. You may consider crossing out information you've covered, particularly if you feel nervous. This way you don't have to worry about accidentally repeating yourself. You may also want to jot down notes as you speak with your contact.

Key Takeaway:
- The more detail you have about the person (things like, their history, accomplishments, and motivations), the easier it will be for you connect with them during an interview or meeting.

CHAPTER EIGHT
COULD I BE THAT PERSON IN 5-7 YEARS?

Applying to every company in sight is tempting, but in order to land your dream internship you must be strategic in your approach. You must be confident in your current ability and aspirations, and you must be able to clearly communicate your experiences to back up your ask.

Informational interviews are a good way to expand your research and develop a better understanding of the industry. Furthermore, you may gain some powerful connections along the way. Some industry insiders remember the difficulty they had when they broke into their fields and will be willing to help you get your foot in the door.

The intention of this hack is to help you identify and connect with professionals who can help you learn more about their industry and help you expand your referral network. From there, you can determine if a certain position is really what you are looking for and if you will be happy interning for that position. You can conduct your exploratory meetings by phone, video conference, or in-person depending on you and your contacts' availability. For this hack you will be using the abbreviated research guide and the LinkedIn Hack so feel free to skip back to review these if necessary.

Your goals for this hack are to

- Find contacts within the industry you are pursuing
- Get to know your contacts
- Expand your network
- Determine if you can see yourself in their shoes in 5-7 years

Start by asking yourself, what is my ultimate goal? Begin to think about your five-year goals. It may seem daunting, but the idea here is that you pursue an internship that puts you on your five-year trajectory. This hack is a roadmap to help you leapfrog your competition.

This process is not one to start a month before you need your internship. This is an iterative process that you must begin months in advance. If you begin to use this hack when you need an internship, people will sense your desperation.

To begin, use your job description master list to find people in each of the fields you chose earlier in the book.

Here are the steps to set up your informational interviews:

1. Research the field(s) you are interested in. Read internship descriptions, understand the salaries etc. (you should have done this in chapter 2).

2. Leverage LinkedIn to find people in the field.

3. Reverse engineer their emails (use LinkedIn Hack).

4. Send a precise email asking for 15 minutes of their time.

5. Research the individual and create template (the previous chapter covers this in great detail).

6. Develop strong questions to ask your contact.

7. Have an in-person conversation or call.

8. Develop a close (how should we stay in touch / can you recommend me to anyone else?).

9. Send them a thank you email the next day.

You must be precise in your ask when you send your initial email. Your contacts are busy and will not do your work for you. Do not say I am looking for a position in IT. That is too broad. Share what you are interested in, some of your experiences, and your skills (see examples below).

The intention of the call or in-person conversation is not necessarily to get an internship, but instead, to learn more about what these professionals do and to determine if you could see yourself in their shoes in 5-7 years from now. Be curious and have a list of questions prepared. Try to reach out to people from all different backgrounds. In other words, speak with both technical and nontechnical people in each field. When you speak to a handful of people in different fields but similar positions, you can begin to assess if the career you have in mind is right for you. You may decide to update your Job Descriptions list with the pertinent information that you gain from these interviews.

Do not ask for an internship during the call or in your follow-up email because it is unfair, manipulative, and you may lose that person as a contact. However, if they do ask if you are looking for an internship, then you may certainly say, "Yes!"

If your conversation goes well, then ask your contact if you can stay in touch. It is so easy to have a conversation and then never speak with them again, but you will be surprised by the number of people who offer to help you out during the process once you establish a connection. Some may even suggest that you take a look at their LinkedIn connections. It's always stronger when an introduction is made for you, so try to get these people on your side. If it feels right, ask them if there is anyone in their network who you could speak to as well.

Before you reach out make sure you have a research guide, general questions regarding their field, and specific questions regarding their experiences. I provide some sample questions below. You don't have to ask every question from your list (you should respect their time), but it is a good idea to be prepared. Also, if you think of questions during the call ask them! Remember the focus is on them and some of your best questions may come up in conversation. Consider the questions you bring and craft beforehand as a starter set to get the ball rolling or as a fall-back if the conversation is going nowhere.

Here are some sample questions:

- What do you do on a day-to-day basis?
- How do you like your current position?
- What challenges do you face?
- What is your favorite and least favorite thing about your current position?
- What do you now know that you wish you knew starting out?

When I was working to land my first internship, many of my initial conversations felt slightly awkward since the contacts didn't know me and I was not applying for an internship per se. However, to break the ice, I would begin each call the same way:

"I really appreciate you taking the time out of your day to chat with me. The intention of the call is for me to learn about you and (the contact's field). I would love to tell you a little bit about myself and then hear about what you do. I also have a list of questions I would like to ask you, but I want to respect your time as well."

Mostly your contacts will appreciate the fact that you are taking their fields seriously when you appear well researched and respectful of their time. Additionally, you will make stronger connections this way because you are reaching out to your contacts to find out about instead of asking what they can do for you.

By using the "Could I be that Person in 5-7 Years Hack?", you have begun to set yourself apart from the competition. Most students love to take action and apply to every internship they see. But few do the grunt work beforehand, and as a result, they miss these meaningful conversations and fail to build a powerful network. By doing the grunt work, you are able to place yourself ahead of the competition.

Aim to create authentic relationships as opposed to transactional relationships, so you can leverage these new connections when the time comes. However, don't force it. If the conversation feels forced and you cannot see yourself speaking with them in the future, be polite and simply send them a thank you email.

Below you will find a few sample email templates:

The cold email (using the LinkedIn Hack)

Dear _____,

I came across you on LinkedIn and was very interested in your expertise.

I am an undergraduate student studying (your major) at (your College/University). I'm exploring different fields specifically in (your field of interest). If you have 15 minutes, I'd love to speak to you about what you do and ask you a few questions.

Best,

_____

Thank you email (the next day after your call or in-person conversation)

Hi _____,

It was great speaking with you today. I appreciate your advice and feedback.
I'll keep in touch.

Best,

_____

If you are lucky enough to get an Introduction, here is a template (make sure to Bcc the person introducing you):

Bill - Thanks for the intro. I'm moving you to Bcc.

Charles - Pleased to e-meet you. Next summer I'm looking to intern and work hard for a company in (your field of interest). I'm a huge fan of (something specific to your field) and (your new connection's company). My passion lies in _____. I'll be available to chat on _____ anytime in the morning or all day _____. Please let me know what would work best for you. I look forward to hearing from you.

Best,

_____

Keep in touch email:

Hi _____,

I wanted to check-in. I completed my Junior Year, and landed an internship with _____ in the _____ department. I hope all is well.

Best,

_____

Key Takeaways:

*   Before you send your first application, you need to do your research.
*   Informational interviews are a good way to expand your research and develop a better understanding of the industry.
*   You need to identify and connect with professionals who can help you learn more about their industry and help you expand your referral network.
*   Determine if you could see yourself in their shoes in 5-7 years from now.
*   Be curious and have a list of questions prepared.

- Always send a thank you following the interview.
- If you don't jive with the person, don't sweat it.

CHAPTER NINE
COVER LETTER HACK

Cover letters can be a great addition to a resume and help you differentiate yourself from others applying for the same internship. Many people skip this step because it's cumbersome to write individual cover letters. Furthermore, there is no guarantee that anyone will read it; however, when you skip a cover letter, you waste a valuable opportunity to add some perspective to your resume.

A cover letter allows you to shape your prospective employers' opinions. It can include things like why you think the position is a good fit and why you think the company would be a great place to work. It also allows you to summarize why your skills will add value if you are chosen. If there are certain skills on your resume that align well with the position, you can say that in your cover letter.

As an employer, I see a lot of resumes and cover letters and there are a few key elements you should keep in mind. Your cover letter should be one page or less and be comprised of a few well-written paragraphs that do the following:

- Describe what position you are applying for and why
- Add context to your resume
- Help an employer understand the value you can bring to his or her business
- Include a few objective accomplishments that relate to the position to add credibility to your points

You can bring a draft of your cover letter to your career advisor or career services office. They understand what recruiters are looking for and can help you make a strong cover letter that enhances your application. It is a good idea to bring a copy of the job description as well.

Note: when you apply electronically, your resume and cover letter should be in the form of a PDF as opposed to doc or docx. Anyone can view a PDF, it provides a cleaner presentation, and it preserves your formatting.

Do not rush your cover letter. Time and time again, I see students sending in a cover letter that never mentions the company's name. These letters typically use "your firm" or "your company." This is sloppy because it's a no brainer to recruiters that you are simply duplicating the cover letter for each company. Even though writing a unique cover letter for every employer takes time, it increases your chances for success, and it shows your interest is genuine.

Here is one example of a rushed cover letter. This is an example of what **not to do** (these cover letters never address the company that he is interested in).

September 14, 2016

To HR,

I am writing to apply for the summer internship at your firm. After speaking to a school advisor, it seems that your firm has a genuine relationship with its employees. I am currently a student studying marketing.

I am someone who seeks challenges, as I look to self-improve daily. My leadership abilities and involvement in school clubs have helped prepare me to develop my professional career in marketing.

I look forward to hearing from you.

Sincerely,
Alex Smith

Below I show you a way to increase your efficiency while still writing a fairly unique cover letter to each of your potential employers.

Cover Letter Template

You may use one cover letter template by industry. Color code the words that you have to remember to change in red – date, the company's mission/values, company industry, and the position. Or separate them from the rest of the letter with parentheses. You may also want to tailor your skill set in the third paragraph so that it incorporates elements of the job description. Using red (or parentheses) allows you mitigate the possibility of writing the wrong industry or even worse, the wrong company name. For company name, do a replace all using the Find and Replace tool on MS Word or Google Docs.

(Company Address)
(Date)

(Company)
RE: (Position)

Dear (Hiring Manager),

(Congratulations on your recent partnership with My Tiny Wins). I have been following (Crony Paleo) for more than a year now and believe I would be a great addition to the team as (a data analyst intern). I am a trained analyst who is detail-oriented and a team player.

Last summer I interned with LIFT Protein Muffins as an Analyst. I collaborated with the management team to identify key customer market segments. Using this information, the marketing team was then proactively able to reach out to prospective customers to increase signup rate by 17 percent.

I believe that my experience in (building and growing a startup, assessing the market, and solving business problems) would benefit (Crony Paleo), serving in the role of a (data analyst intern). In short, I believe I would be an asset to (Crony Paleo), since I align with (Crony Paleo's values of demonstrating integrity and commitment, as well as collaborating with people of different backgrounds.)

Sincerely,

_____

What if I mess up and send a cover letter using the wrong company's name?

You have three options. Just move on and throw that application out the window. Chances are they won't say anything or give you a hard time. If they do, apologize and learn from your mistake. The second option is to re-send the application after you realize your mistake and then let them know. They still may not take you seriously, but there is no harm in trying.

Your best option, however, is to utilize the Undo Tool in Gmail which allows you to quickly unsend a message you have already sent. This tool is a lifesaver. Here's how to set it up:

1. Click the gear in the top right of your Gmail inbox.
2. Select Settings.
3. Scroll down to "Undo Send" and click Enable.
4. Set the cancellation period (the amount of time you have to decide if you want to unsend an email).
5. Click Save Changes at the bottom of the page.

If you use Google Inbox, this feature is already integrated. Click on "Cancel" and it will undo your email.

I once sent the wrong email to a potential employer a few years ago using the wrong name! I was introduced to an individual who was going to connect me to a few employers. I used a cover letter template but forgot to change his name. I did not know about undo send at the time. After I sent it, I realized what I had done. I sent him a follow-up email profusely apologizing. I was hoping he would just push it aside. Instead, he decided to call me and lecture me on respect and then told the person who introduced us, and that person then sent me a furious email. I felt horrible, but at this point, I decided to scrap both individuals and continue the search. This, of course, is an extreme case, and I hope it never happens to you.

Key Takeaways:

- Include the company name, its mission or values, and any recent news from the firm on your cover letter.
- Look at the internship description for keywords that you can use for your cover letter.
- To make this simple, you can highlight keywords in red on your template, so you can easily swap out keywords based on what the employer is looking for.

CHAPTER TEN
SEARCH COMPANIES HACK (APPLYING)

In this hack, we walk you through the process of applying for internships. All of the prep work you have done so far leads up to this moment. With that said, if you don't feel like you have built a strong enough referral base, you may want to skip ahead to the Meetup and Albert's List hacks and return to this afterward when you are ready to begin applying.

By the time you begin this hack, you have a clear understanding of what types of roles you are interested in pursuing for your internship. You may not be 100% set on the type of role, but because of the Research Job

Descriptions Hack, you should know generally where your interests lie and what skills you are interested in developing. Also, by now you should have networked and developed an understanding of the internship's functionalities and requirements. Before you begin, be sure to refer to your notes and compile your list of connections.

To begin, find several job search sites to use. Some search sites include: The Muse, LinkedIn Jobs, Indeed, AngelList, and a niche Facebook job group called Albert's List (discussed in Chapter 12).

Then, set up a plan to stay organized. It is essential to stay organized so you can see who you have and have not yet contacted on your list. The list also gives you a sense of accomplishment as you mark off the employers you've contacted.

To make sure you remain organized, create a spreadsheet similar to the example below. The first column should contain the list of companies you want to contact. In the second column, indicate what employee from the company you plan to reach out to. In the third column, list the employee's position. The fourth column should contain the position that you are applying for. You may also add companies to your spreadsheet that you are passionate about even if they may not have openings at the time. Once you contact the employee, highlight the row yellow. If you get an offer, highlight the row green. If you get a rejection, highlight it in red.

Company Name	Employee Name	Employee Position	Interested Position
LIFT Protein Muffins	Zachary Schleien	Director of Marketing	Business Analyst Intern
The Work Book	Bill Hobbs	Director of Marketing	Business Analyst Intern
My Tiny Wins	John Doe	Marketing Associate	Marketing Associate Intern
Crony Paleo	Michelle Smith	Business Intelligence Analyst	Business Intelligence Intern

You will also want to make one folder called "Internship," (see page 88) which will contain your resume, cover letters, and your master list of companies. Make a second folder called "Applied." In the "Applied" folder, create a folder for each company that you have applied to. These folders will also contain your cover letter and any other documents that are unique for that employer. Keep your resume and transcript in the Internship folder as well, so you can get to it easily when you're applying.

Once you have applied to several companies, it is time to start leveraging LinkedIn to connect with your future bosses.

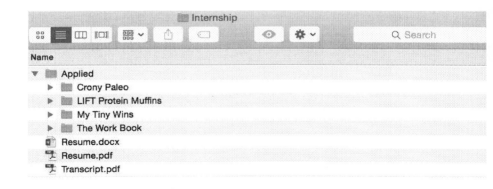

How to leverage LinkedIn

Upgrade your LinkedIn to premium. LinkedIn offers a free one-month trial. If you have used it in the past, you may want to purchase it during your internship search. It brings your application to the top of the list and offers some nifty features called, Premium Insights. Premium insights show the number of applicants who have applied to the position, the estimated salary for that position, the education level of applicants, the top skills, the seniority of applicants, etc.

After you apply for an internship, reach out to one of your connections who knows someone in the company. Asking for introductions is one of the reasons LinkedIn was created. In order to see if you have any connections linked to someone in the company, search the company you applied to in LinkedIn.

1. Set the search bar to "companies" and search for the company you applied to.
2. Then click "see all".
3. Scroll through the individuals, and find the employee's job title that has the potential to hire you.
4. Determine if you are connected to the individual. If you aren't try to find someone who is. If you can't do that, then skip ahead to the section titled "What to do if you have no first connections."

If there are too many employees to scroll through, you can do a search in LinkedIn for company name and then search the job title of your future boss, for example, Crony Paleo and then Marketing Director. From there you can hopefully pinpoint your future boss.

It is always best if you can ask for an introduction, as introductions are much stronger than cold emailing your future boss. A warm introduction is more likely to yield results. Cold intros are an important part of the process, but warm introductions will allow you more flexibility because they invoke a basic human principle called social proof.

In the scenario below, I determined who my future boss would be in the role I was applying for. I applied for a Marketing Coordinator internship. From there, I went on LinkedIn and did a quick search and identified the Director of Customer Acquisition. I then saw how we were connected and sent the message shown below.

Hi Bill,

Hope all is well. I noticed you are connected to Charles Smith from Crony Paleo. I applied for the Marketing Coordinator Internship and was wondering if you would be able to make an intro.

Best,
Zach

Power of the LinkedIn Introduction (another example)

In the example below. I view Samantha Roberts' profile on LinkedIn. LinkedIn displays how I am connected to Samantha, with Samantha being a 2nd connection. In fact, Mike Young is a 1st connection. I can then reach out to Mike asking for a introduction to Samantha.

Zach Schleien → Mike Young (1st connection) → Samantha Roberts (2nd connection)

Hey Mike,

Hope all is well. I noticed that you are connected to Samantha Roberts from Crony Paleo. I applied for the marketing internship. I was wondering if you could make an introduction?

Best,
Zach

(Don't be surprised if they email you, saying intern with my company!)

Hey Zach,

Yes, but first...definitely take a look at LIFT Protein

We're blowing up, and would love for you to get onboard!

Mike

What to do if you have no first connections:

If you have no 1st connections to that individual, you can cold email the individual using the LinkedIn Hack (return to this chapter if you need a refresher). You should email them as opposed to InMailing them on LinkedIn, since LinkedIn offers only a handful of InMails to premium users. With email, you can reach out to anyone!

If no intro is made within 3-5 days, ping your contact again. Of course, be respectful. Here is an example below.

Hi Mike,

Did you have a chance to see if Samantha Roberts would be interested in connecting?

Zach

One of the hardest parts is just getting started, but once you do, you may be surprised that you thoroughly enjoy applying and put in the hard work to land your next internship. Take advantage of this opportunity. You may have the opportunity to apply to internships anywhere in the country or even the world.

What to do if there are no internships at the company?

If there are no applicable internships on the company's career page, indicate that on your spreadsheet with the date. If it is a company you would love to intern with, come back and do a search a couple of weeks later. You can also email someone from the company, (your future boss or a recruiter) express your interest, and say you went on the job board but there was no position that aligned with your skills.

Try to establish a relationship with someone within the company, and make sure that person understands that you really love the company and would like to check back. If he or she agrees, you can check in periodically to see if there are any internships or special projects that you can help with. When the opening comes up, you may be surprised that the person pings you, or you ping him or her, and the person appreciates your follow-up and tenacity. You may want to set a calendar invite to do a search on the company's career page or set up a reminder in your Google Inbox app so the message appears a few weeks later.

It is important to set time aside in your calendar to apply for internships, email the head of HR, and email your "future boss". It is also important to set aside time to ask your LinkedIn connections for introductions after you have applied for internships. Setting a time in your calendar holds you responsible and helps you avoid procrastination.

Email your future boss at various times during the week. Avoid emailing them on Friday evening or on the weekend. If they don't respond, feel free to make a reminder in your mailbox app or calendar to follow up in a week or two. Don't overdo it.

What if you have no connections and can't figure out your "future boss's" email?

One of your remaining options is to tweet at the connection with something relating to his or her tweets and interests.

Here are some examples you may find useful:

Bill,

I'm an avid user of LIFT Protein Muffins. I applied for the Data Analyst Intern position. I came across you on LinkedIn and was very interested in your expertise.

I am an undergraduate student in the Marketing Program at Syracuse University. My passion lies in community engagement and digital marketing. During college I co-founded a startup company. Recently, I launched a blog called MyTinyWins.com, where I manage our analytics, drive growth, and write the majority of the content.

This January my goals are to contribute to a tech company as well as to be in a strong learning environment. Given my experiences, I know I can be a valuable asset to your company. I know you are busy, but if you have some time to chat over the phone or grab coffee, I would really appreciate it. I can be contacted at zschlei@syr.edu and reached at (555) 555-

5555. My resume is attached.

Best,
Zach

You can even email companies that don't have internship openings, but for which you have a true calling.

Bill and Charles,

I am absolutely in love with LIFT Protein Muffins. Your company embodies my values of health and nutrition.

I am a rising senior from Syracuse University with a Degree in Marketing. I would love the opportunity to speak with both of you about a possible internship opportunity with LIFT Protein Muffins. My passion lies in data analysis, digital marketing, and growth.

Last summer I interned with Crony Paleo as a Marketing Data Analyst where I analyzed data to identify customers most at risk for churn. More recently, I launched a blog called MyTinyWins.com. I have grown

MyTinyWins.com from an idea to a bustling blog that now receives 18,000 unique views/month.

I know I would be an incredible asset to LIFT Protein Muffins. Please find my resume attached.

Best,
Zach

Key Takeaways:
- Stay organized.
- Utilize LinkedIn's free one-month premium trial.
- If you have no 1st or 2nd connections with the individual you are interested in contacting, you can cold email that individual using the LinkedIn Hack.
- Introductions are much stronger than cold emailing your "future boss" or recruiter, but cold emailing is a necessary part of the process. After all, you can't be connected to everybody!

CHAPTER ELEVEN
MEETUP
HACK

You can get hired through a job board or career fair, but the best way to land an internship is through a referral. And the best way to get a referral is to spend time building relationships. The hack highlighted below is another way to continue building your network and in turn, get referred for an ideal internship opportunity.

First, it is important to know that "Firms often use referrals from existing employees to hire new workers: about 50% of U.S. jobs are found through informal networks and about 70% of firms have programs encouraging referral-based hiring."[3]

3 Burks, Stephen V. et. al. pp. 805-806

One great way to continue building your referral network is to attend Meetup events. Meetup.com is a website where you can meet people who share your interests. For example, if you would like to land an internship in the digital marketing field, then you can go to digital marketing Meetups. It is the perfect, low-pressure opportunity to make connections and build your network.

Before attending a Meetup, browse the website to see which Meetups interest you and align with your career objectives. Once you join 5 or more Meetups, look at the upcoming schedule. Meetup.com aggregates your Meetups and will show you what Meetups take place where, on which day, and at what time. You should attend Meetups in the location you would like to work because it increases your chances of developing a connection who can refer you to an internship. If you don't have class every day of the week, set aside some time in your schedule to attend a few Meetups. If you can't take off from school, there is an alternative; browse the Meetup attendee list. It is not as effective as attending a Meetup event, but it is better than taking no action!

Let's say you go to Syracuse University, and you

can't make a digital marketing Meetup in NYC. You could always go to Meetups in Syracuse, but they will not be as valuable to you as those in NYC. Instead of getting discouraged, browse the attendee list for the NYC Meetup. Research the attendees on LinkedIn. You can also view their bios in their Meetup profile. If their skills and profession align with your career objectives, shoot them an email using the Reverse Engineer Email Hack. You could email them over Meetup, but doing so is riskier because they may rarely check their Meetup account. Be transparent in your email, and let them know that you came across them by browsing the Meetup, but unfortunately, you cannot attend. Invite them on a Skype or phone call. And if you hit it off, try to meet with them in-person when you have time.

Don't skip class to attend a Meetup because there is always a risk that you will not gain much value from the meeting. Furthermore, you don't want to become overwhelmed because you have missed too many classes.

If you can attend Meetups, be sure to do your research prior to attending.

Start by creating a "People You Would Like to

Meet at the Meetup Event" document.

1. Review the attendee list.
2. Read their Meetup.com bios.
3. If the bio doesn't interest you, skip to the next individual.
4. If the bio does interest you, search for the person on LinkedIn.
5. If your skill-sets align, add the attendee to your document. Include the person's name, photo, title and any other relevant career facts.
6. Use the Reverse Engineer Email Hack to obtain their emails and send them each a short email.

Example Email / Meetup message

Hi Bill - I noticed that you will be attending the Digital Marketing Meetup event on October 29th. I'd love the opportunity to connect. See you then!

Sometimes people will say that they will be in attendance, but they do not show. If you miss a connection, set up a time to grab coffee with them instead.

After you compile your document, study your list of attendees. You don't have to memorize everyone. However, you should familiarize yourself with the document so you can quickly identify each attendee at the Meetup. When you see them, share with them that you wanted to meet. Not only will this boost their ego, but they will also be impressed with your preparation.

Once you arrive to the Meetup event, be social. Introduce yourself to everyone and have your elevator pitch prepared. Attend Meetups even if you are unable to convince your friends to come with you. It is perfectly natural to feel uncomfortable because you don't know anyone there, but view the Meetup as an opportunity to build your network. The more people you don't know, the greater your chances are to meet a valuable bridge or better yet, someone who could offer you an internship.

Also, keep in mind that everyone is most likely just as uncomfortable as you are. Once you "break the ice" and open the door for conversation, the tough part is over, and people will happily engage with you. The key is to be the one breaking the ice and making others feel comfortable. Some easy openers include: chatting about the weather, asking what brought people to the event, how long have they been attending Meetups, or what do they do for a living. These are very simple openers and don't require others to engage too deeply in conversation if they don't want to. On the other hand, intros like these break the ice and allow for a natural progression towards conversation.

One trick I use to motivate myself is the 3-second rule. Pretend you have 3 seconds to approach someone you don't know. In reality, if you wait too long, you can become frazzled, and it becomes much more difficult to reach out.

It is okay to have your Meetup list out, but don't make it too visible while scouting for your attendees. The new contact you are meeting may ask, "What do you do?" If you are a student, you may not be able to say that you work for an employer, but you still can sell yourself. Share with them that you are a student studying your major, you do these extracurricular activities, and you are looking for an internship in this desired field and are attending to build contacts in the industry. This shows that you are prepared and have a goal in mind. Your goal is to get these people to help you get an interview at their company or help you connect with someone within your field of interest. And as a bonus, if someone you meet is looking for an intern, you already have your elevator pitch ready to go.

It is also imperative that you introduce yourself to the organizer. The organizers often have the largest network of connections and are the most willing to help you expand your own network. Also, the organizer may highlight new attendees and what they do. They may ask you to introduce yourself to the group in which case, you have an immediate platform in which to sell yourself.

Here is an example Meetup document:

Bill: The WORK Book

Bill is an author

Zach: Lift Protein Muffins

Zach runs Marketing and Growth

My Meetup Successes

I went to a food tech pitch competition Meetup that began with a pitch competition. The judges then rewarded the top company pitch. Following the competition there was a networking opportunity. Before I attended the event, I reviewed the presenters and judges. I made sure to learn about the judges beforehand. The founders of the food tech companies were mobbed following their presentation but the judges were not. Once the competition concluded and the networking event began, I introduced myself to one of the judges. I read up on him prior to the event.

I shared with him a little about my paleo muffin company and he told me he was curious about the paleo diet, since it was a market opportunity to introduce paleo into his company. In addition to the muffin conversation, I shared with him that I had worked on some data initiatives for my last startup. We connected on LinkedIn, and I shared with him that I was looking for a full-time opportunity following graduation. He said his company was looking to take someone on who had a passion for strategy and analytics, and he asked me to send him my resume.

In networking, persistence is important. It took over a month with back and forth email conversations for me to finally meet with one of the other contacts I made. I stayed persistent and was polite throughout the email exchange. When we finally connected, he told me about a position that I would be interested in. Again, always be respectful even if they don't email you after several consecutive emails. You may eventually have to give up, but more times than not, people are willing to help out. Here is an example of a follow up email I used.

Hi Bill,

It was great meeting you at the Syracuse event! I'd love to grab a coffee or a quick bite after work sometime before I head back to Syracuse. Are you available any day from August 10-12th?

Best,
Zach

Note: As an intern, you should continue to use the

Meetup hack especially if you are interning in the city where you would like to work full-time. You should want to continue to build your network even as you are interning.

Key Takeaways:
- Before attending a Meetup, browse the website to see which Meetups interest you and align with your career objectives.
- Create a "People You Would Like to Meet at The Meetup Event" document.
- You should attend Meetups in the location where you would like to work because it increases your chances of developing a connection who can refer you to an internship.
- Once you arrive to the Meetup event, be social.
- Use the 3-second rule! You have 3 seconds to approach someone you don't know.
- Introduce yourself to the organizers.

CHAPTER TWELVE
ALBERT'S LIST

By now, you understand the power of referrals. Another great tool for building a referral network is Albert's List. Albert's List is a Facebook group that connects recruiters and internship seekers. When I posted a question to the network, people were extremely responsive and willing to help. Positions are primarily based in California; however, you can still get advice or a referral for another location. As an internship seeker, you can ask for advice, referrals, or an opportunity to network. You can join the group regardless of your internship location preference. When you reach out, make sure to be concise and explicit about what you are looking for.

In other words, do not say "I am looking for an internship! Advice needed." A post like this is way too generic and gives no background on who you are or where your skills lie. A clear and concise example is provided below.

Here is the link:

https://www.facebook.com/groups/findyournextopportunity/

[Seeking Full-time Opportunity - NY metropolitan area]

Hi Everyone!

I am currently receiving a BS in Marketing from Syracuse University (Dec '15). Last summer I interned at LIFT Protein Muffins as a Data Analyst.

My passion and skill-set is in digital marketing. I am an excellent communicator with a love for analytics! My goal is to secure an internship in the New York metropolitan area. If you are hiring or can refer me to someone who is, that would be a huge help!

Here is my LinkedIn:
https://www.linkedin.com/in/zacharyschleien

Skills I Would Like to Develop:
- Track business metrics and provide actionable insights
- Google Analytics, Excel
- R programming
- Interpersonal and communication skills
- Analyze & measure marketing ROI
- Drive user acquisition
- A/B testing
- Optimization

Notice that in the example above I am specific about what I am studying and what I am asking for. Make it as easy as possible on the people who could potentially help you by keeping your post specific and precise.

CHAPTER THIRTEEN
VENTURE CAPITAL HACK

Finding companies that are actually hiring can be tough if they aren't actively advertising openings. In the startup world companies often begin to scale their teams after they raise capital. One place to find out who has Venture Capital is to scour sites such as CB Insights.

Main Resource:

CB Insights: a venture capital database and angel investment database that provides daily, real-time information about venture capital. Register for CB Insights with a company email, and you will get a 30-day free trial. You can explore the site and play around with the filters. Narrow down your results by location, industry, or last funding date. From there you will have a list of companies that you can apply to. CB Insights only allows for a limited number of searches before you have to request a demo. If you run out, then you can use any of the other resources listed below. Check it out at www.cbinsights.com

CrunchBase

CrunchBase is a free website that helps you to discover companies that interest you. The site offers a daily feed which details company news and investment deals. You can use these company facts to demonstrate your credibility in your cover letter or when you reach out. Aside from the feed, you have the ability to discover detailed company information with CrunchBase's powerful search feature. You can search for companies based off of the amount of money they raised, the number of employees, their founding date, and location.

In addition to helping you discovering companies, CrunchBase is a valuable resource to help you find nearby events. Under the "Events" tab you can browse Conferences and Networking Events to further build your referral network.

For $29 a month you can also access Crunch-Base Pro, which offers more advanced search capabilities. You can get started with CrunchBase here www. crunchbase.com.

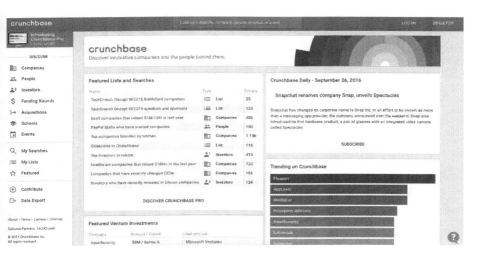

Other Resources:

Silicon Tap - www.silicontap.com - High technology and deal news for Silicon Valley.

Venture Beat - venturebeat.com/category/deals - Technology trends and news.

CHAPTER FOURTEEN
HACKS, RITUALS, & ROUTINES BEFORE AN INTERVIEW

By this point in the book, you should have built a pretty extensive referral network, applied to several internships, and scheduled several interviews. You may be excited and nervous the night before a big interview but that's okay. Here are several hacks, rituals, and routines to help you prepare before an interview. You may find some or all of them helpful before your interview.

- Eat well before the interview.
- Do your prep work the night before. Print your resume, have your questions prepared, and be sure

to complete your research on the company and interviewer before the day of. If you have already finished all of your prep work, then review it! Don't wait to do these things the morning of, since your objective on interview day is to focus on the interview and not things you forgot to complete.

- Print out multiple resumes. Chances are they will have your resume on file once you arrive, but from time to time, the interviewer may ask for an updated resume. Make sure to print out your resume the night before and put it in a folder to maintain its condition. Sometimes others from the company will be pulled in last minute to your interview so having extra resumes is always a good idea.

- Ask the recruiter or hiring manager the format of the interview before your interview. Knowing the format can help you prepare. If it's a technical interview, figure out if it will include a test like a coding drill. If it's a consulting interview, you may want to read up on case studies. If it's for sales, figure out if you'll be tested on selling skills or presentation skills. You get the idea.

- Be sure to read up on news about the company and

any world events that may help you to connect with the business climate before the interview.

- Begin to brainstorm questions to ask your interviewer prior to the interview. It is important to begin to think about questions and get into the right mindset, even if you may not ask them during the interview. It will also give you some material to fall back on if you can't think of any questions during the interview.

- Give yourself ample preparation time prior to the interview.

- Review your notes. If you arrive early, you can review your notes in a nearby coffee shop or in the lounge at the interview location.

- Bring a pen and notepad. You may not remember all of the answers to your questions during the interview, so bring a pen and notepad. Take notes on what the position entails, jot down your answers to the questions you receive, etc. As an added bonus, you may find that taking notes while you speak helps you focus your responses and plan ahead.

Key Takeaways:

- Give yourself ample time prior to the interview.
- Review your notes.
- Take notes during your interview.

CHAPTER FIFTEEN
ACE THE INTERVIEW HACK

For some students, the interview is the most challenging, nerve-racking part of the internship process. However, if you come prepared, the interview should be the most exciting part of the process (prior to landing your internship, of course!).

Here are 7 tips to help you ace the interview:

1. The Handshake: If you are sitting and your interviewer walks into the room, stand up to shake his or her hand. Be sure to make eye contact while you shake hands. Do the same at the conclusion of the

interview. It is important to stand up if you are sitting because it shows your interviewers respect.

2. Start with Small Talk: Whether you are on a phone interview or an in-person interview, it is important to create a rapport with the interviewer through small talk. Greet your interviewers, and spark up a conversation. Ask them how they are doing, and when they ask you the same, share with them something positive about how you are doing.

Note: Though it is rare, some interviewers may want to jump straight into the interview and skip the small talk. Be sure to follow these cues and adjust appropriately.

3. Communication Starts with Listening: Before you answer any question, listen closely to ensure you understand the question. If you need clarification, don't be afraid to ask.

4. Share Good Stories: Your interviewers will likely ask you about experiences you have had. They may ask you to talk about a time when you failed, or discuss

a project you led and what you learned from leading it. When you answer these types of questions, share stories that illustrate your strengths and experience. More information can be found in The WORK Book : How to Build Your Personal Brand and Get Hired!

5. Pay Full Attention: It is important to be aware and present during your interview. Focus only on the interview and don't let outside distractions draw your attention.

6. Treat Your Interview Like a Conversation: Rather than trying to impress your interviewer, focus on answering his or her questions thoroughly and share your experiences. Interviews should feel more like a conversation than a one-sided Q & A. You should feel free to ask questions too.

7. Do Your Research: Know your facts about the company. Read about the position you are interviewing for and your interviewer's background. Stay up on current news about the company and industry and

be prepared to discuss.

Here are some good questions to ask:
- What types of projects will I be working on over the summer?
- What types of skills will I learn?
- Is there an opportunity that the position will translate to a full-time role? If so, what will that take?
- What does the training/on-boarding process look like?
- What makes someone great in the position I am interviewing for?
- What are the long-term and short term goals of the company?
- How does this role contribute to the company's goals?
- What metrics would you use to measure success in this role?
- What are some of the challenges or roadblocks one might come up against in this role?

Key Takeaways:
- Shake hands.

- Start with small talk.
- Communication starts with listening.
- Share stories.
- Stay focused.
- Treat your interview like a conversation.
- Do your research.

CHAPTER SIXTEEN
THE FOLLOW-UP GAME

One of the most important things you can do after an interview is follow up. It not only shows your interest level in the opportunity, but tactically, it is one of the most important things you can do because it keeps you fresh in the interviewer's mind.

If you are apprehensive about following up, one way to make the process seamless is to set expectations before leaving the interview. This way you and the interviewer have agreed on a time for you to check back in. Then when you follow up, you remind the hiring manager about moving things forward and demonstrate that you keep your word. At the end of the interview, you can bring up the next steps and write down the action items. As part of this process, simply ask your interviewers the best way to follow up with them.

Here are four easy steps to effective follow-ups:

Step 1: At the end of the interview ask, "How should I follow up?"

Step 2: Send a thank you email or thank you card on following day of your interview.

Step 3: Follow-up with your interviewer on the agreed upon time.

Step 4: If you don't hear back after a few days, reach out again.

Try to follow the internal process during the initial interview. Don't call the office if you have to apply online. Many companies have specific processes they follow for hiring that require steps to be completed in a specific order. It is important to follow the process they lay out so you do not annoy them. In other words, if they ask you not to call, then don't call. If they ask you to fill out paperwork or take an assessment before the interview, be sure to complete everything beforehand.

If the employer does not follow up with you after the interview, don't shy away from contacting them. Be polite and persistent, but follow the process. It may take one or more emails to finally reconnect.

If you get the feeling that they will never return your email, it is okay to sometimes give up. You may feel that you wasted effort and that the interviewer is being inconsiderate; sometimes it happens. Move on. There are more opportunities out there

When you do write the follow-up email, make sure it is specific. Don't say "I wanted to check-in", but rather "You had asked me to touch base with you in August." As always, be specific.

Here are some templates to help guide you:

Hi _____,

I'm writing to follow up on our last conversation. You

had asked me to touch base sometime in (Month). Could we schedule a call to reconnect next _____ at __am or _____ at __?

Best,

_____

Following up after an interview or meeting some-one in-person

Dear _____,

Great meeting you yesterday! I'm excited about (the company's) direction and the upcoming (news). I look forward to reconnecting in July.

Best,

_____,

Hi _____,

Great meeting you today! Attached is a copy of my reume. I look forward to speaking with you in the next two weeks.

Best,

_____

Following up with someone who's connected you to someone in their network

Hi _____,

Great meeting you today! Please find my resume attached.

I am passionate about customer acquisition with a strong background in analytics. I consider myself to be entrepreneurial, having worked on two startups and a blog.

Thanks again!

_____

Following up during the summer or simply to stay

in touch

Hi _____,

Hope you are having a great summer! My internship at _____ is winding down, and I would love the opportunity to meet with you before I head back to (your school). Please let me know if you're around next week.

Best,

_____

Following up to obtain a contact's number

Hi _____,

(this time) on (the day) would be perfect! What is the best phone number to reach you?

Best,

_____

Key Takeaways:

- At the end of the interview, ask the best way to follow up.
- Send a thank you email or thank you card on following day of your interview.
- Follow-up with your interviewer on the agreed upon time.
- If you don't hear back after a few days, reach out again.

CHAPTER SEVENTEEN
CANCELLATION & HOW TO AVOID IT

The worst feeling in the world is traveling to meet someone only to find out that they have to cancel on you and didn't notify you that they couldn't make it.

I used the Reverse Engineer Email Hack to have a phone call with someone who is the director of analytics at an eCommerce company. We planned to meet in the city to have an informal interview over lunch.

When I arrived, I got a table. I stood around for 15 minutes and then shot him an email. After 45 minutes, he still hadn't arrived, so I left. I finally received an email:

He replied, "Um... really sorry, I totally missed this. I thought we were trying to confirm a spot and lost track of it. Are you still around?"

By the time he responded, I had left the city. It was a terrible feeling, but from this experience, I learned three valuable lessons.

- First, send your contact a calendar invite.
- Second, get your contact's telephone number.
- Third, confirm the meeting the day before.

Reminding your contacts of your meetings and getting their telephone numbers will help you avoid being stood up. There is no complete failsafe to cancellations but you should try to take the steps above to decrease the possibility.

CHAPTER EIGHTEEN
YOU HAVE MULTIPLE OFFERS. NOW WHAT?

O nce you land multiple internship offers, you are in the clear! Your hard work has paid off, and you are now in the driver's seat. Below are a few factors to consider before choosing between your internship offers.

Do you have a future? Arguably the most important factor to consider is whether or not you have a future at that company? An internship can be an opportunity to extend into a full-time position following your graduation. These questions can be addressed during the interview process or afterward when you are considering accepting a position.

Pay. Depending on your financial situation, pay may be a big factor when you choose an internship. Pay can also depend on the industry and your skill set. You will have to decide how important pay is as a criterion.

According to Glassdoor the national average internship salary is $33,120 as of August 10, 2016.[4]

Learning. Where is the greatest opportunity to learn? An internship is an opportunity to learn and to develop your existing skills. It is imperative to ask what type of projects you will be working on. If the company is indirect, unclear, or the project does not allow you to hone the skills you wish to develop, you may choose to join another company.

Size. How big or small is the company? Will you be working on a team or solo? With a lot or a little supervision? How many roles will you have? Determining these factors can play into your decision.

Can you build relationships? It is essential to con-

---

[4] "Intern Salaries"

tinue to build relationships once you begin your internship. If your role is to work by yourself all summer, you may have some difficulty building relationships, especially if you are working remotely. If you aren't working remotely, you can still use your breaks and lunches to network.

Brand. Following your internship, you may need to start the interview process all over again. Having a recognized brand on your resume can help distinguish you from other applicants on future jobs. Consider how a strong corporate brand may help you when seeking full-time employment, but this shouldn't be the single factor guiding your decision.

Ask trusted confidants. Ask friends, family, and people in the industry their thoughts on which internship to go with. Some of these people may have been through the process already. It is also important to ask them why when they give you an answer so you understand why they are pointing you in a specific direction. They may help you see your opportunities from a different point of view. Ultimately the decision is yours, but having other's opinions will help you make a more informed decision.

Go with your gut. Never overlook what your gut says. If an internship opportunity just doesn't feel right and you have other offers that feel better, go with one of those offers instead. Oftentimes, your gut will point you in the right direction even if everyone says otherwise.

Glassdoor. Look at glassdoor.com reviews and ratings. If one company is rated a 2.8 while the other is a 4.2, drill down into reviews by job function. If you are interviewing for a sales internship, it may be possible that the sales team on the 2.8 rated company had more positive reviews and ratings then the 4.2 rated company.

Lists. If you are really having trouble deciding, you can make a pros and cons list to help you decide which company to choose.

Key Takeaways:
- Ask friends, family, and people in the industry their thoughts on which internship to go with.
- Never overlook what your gut says.
- Look at glassdoor.com reviews and ratings.

CHAPTER NINETEEN
ONCE YOU FINALIZE YOUR INTERNSHIP

Once you have chosen your company and accepted your internship, respectfully notify the other companies that gave you offers. Don't forget to inform the other people who helped you during the process as well. In order to follow up with everyone, look at all your master list of contacts. Once you let them know, you may consider staying in touch with them. They could be helpful with your future endeavors. Avoid falling off the face of the earth without ever notifying them because your goal is to build long-term relationships, even if those relationships are simply an occasional check-in or coffee. People want to help and be acknowledged when they do.

If anyone went out of their way to help you or if he or she was the person that connected you to the company that you are interning for, consider sending that person a gift. Do some investigation on Twitter to see what his or her interests are. Acknowledge those who helped you along the way and try build long-term relationships with them. These are the connections you should not squander.

Examples:

Stay in touch template

Hi _____,

I really appreciate you meeting with me again. I decided to take a position with _____ in their _____ rotation. I would love to keep in touch.

Best,

_____

Rejection to other company email template

Hi _____,

Thank you again for the offer. This morning I was offered an internship with_____, which included compensation. I decided to take their offer. Again, it was great meeting you and your team and good luck to (your company).

Best,

_____

Key Takeaways:

- Once you choose your company, respectfully notify the other companies that gave you offers.
- Don't forget to inform the other people who helped you during the process as well.

CONCLUSION

Now that you have closed the loop with all of your contacts and successfully landed the internship of your dreams, take a moment to celebrate and congratulate yourself. It is a great accomplishment and marks the beginning of your new professional life!

As we discussed throughout the book, an internship is a key component to building a strong personal brand that will ultimately allow you to differentiate yourself from others when you are ready to seek full-time employment. In order to ensure that you have a great experience in your new internship, you should spend some time creating a plan for success, understanding what to do and what to avoid in your new role, and learning how to effectively communicate your ideas within your new organization.

This planning falls outside the scope of what we cover in this book, but it is discussed in great detail in another WORK Book Series book by Bill Hobbs, called The WORK Book: How to Build Your Personal Brand and Get Hired! bit.ly/TheWORKBook

During and after your internship, don't lose sight of the value of the experience. You should enjoy it and learn all that you can. Remember to continue growing your network inside the company and within the rest of the industry and to continue connecting with employers and pitching yourself. Work hard, be punctual, enthusiastic, and do the best work you possibly can for your new company. You may have to make sacrifices, but this is your future and it is up to you to do what is most important to you. There may be obstacles along way, you may be rejected, you might even have friends land internships before you, but always stay positive and focused on your goals. An internship will not only be a great experience for you, it will help shape the future of your professional career!

These hacks are useful beyond internships, so continue to use this book as you begin your professional career.

APPENDIX

Here we provide a more detailed explanation of the apps mentioned in the introduction and throughout the book.

iCal, Google Calendar, Outlook

A calendar app is the most important app for you to utilize when hacking the internship process. When you have to make edits to your cover letter, research employers, or do some reverse engineering of emails, put it on your calendar. Instead of storing it in your head, write down the task to keep yourself accountable and prevent the someday syndrome.

When you schedule an interview, write it down in your calendar with the phone number and any directions or reminders and add an alert beforehand. You then have no excuse to ever be late.

Hacks this applies to: all

Google Inbox

Google Inbox is an essential tool for your success. The app has numerous useful features. One of which is Reminders. If you need to follow up with an employer or need a reminder to apply for a position on a specific date, use the reminder function in Google Inbox.

Another valuable feature is Snooze. Snooze allows you to come back to an email or reminder at a later date. In other words, when you Snooze an email or reminder, it disappears from your inbox and resurfaces on the designated date or at the location you've set. This capability allows you to stay organized.

Google Inbox also has Bundles which group similar emails together. For example, when you travel for an interview, Bundles will group all flights, hotels, and other relevant information together to help you to stay organized during your trip. Once you make a flight, it will sync the dates and information with your Google calendar.

Another important function of Google Inbox is the Undo Tool. If you accidentally send an email that you didn't intend to send, you can use Google's Undo Tool to unsend your email (as long as you don't wait too long). Check it out at www.google.com/inbox

Hacks this applies to: The Follow-up Game, Cover Letter, Could I be that Person in 5-7 Years?, Search Companies Hack

A Notebook

The notebook, a seemingly obsolete tool in the modern age, still offers you many advantages. You don't have to worry about your notebook crashing. You don't have to wait for it to boot. Plus, physically writing down what you need to do can help you remember things, stay organized, and stay on task. Additionally, notepads are quick and reliable. Write down your most important tasks of the day the night before in the order of importance.

Hacks this applies to: all

Rapportive

Rapportive is a free app found on the Google Chrome store that syncs LinkedIn with Gmail. This tool is used to reverse engineer an employer's email. Rapportive can reveal an employer's email once you guess it correctly. This app will be used throughout the hacks in this book. Check it out at rapportive.com

Hacks this apples to: LinkedIn Hack, Could I be that Person in 5-7 Years?, Search Companies Hack

Yesware

Yesware is a tool for Gmail that allows you to see when a recipient opens your email and how many times that recipient has viewed it. There are a few other cool features available as well. Check it out at www.yesware.com

Hacks this applies to: LinkedIn Hack, Could I be that

Person in 5-7 Years?, Search Companies Hack, to name a few

Boomerang Respondable

Boomerang, a plugin for Gmail and Outlook and most known for its schedule email feature, has released Boomerang Respondable. Free to use, Respondable will predict how likely your message is to receive a response. The response scale ranges from "Very Unlikely" to "Very Likely". In order to determine the likelihood of an email reply, Boomerang takes into account parameters such as, subject length, word count, question count, and reading level.

If you want to fully leverage its capabilities you can upgrade to the Pro version for $14.99/month where you can view advanced parameters such as positivity, politeness, and subjectivity.

Check out Boomerang Respondable:
Gmail: www.boomeranggmail.com/respondable
Outlook: www.boomerangoutlook.com/respondable

Hacks this applies to: LinkedIn Hack, Could I be that

Person in 5-7 Years?, Search Companies Hack

Evernote

Evernote is an electronic notepad for all of your ideas. You can download it for free on your phone and computer. Use Evernote to prep before an interview or to take notes following an interview. Check it out at evernote.com

Hacks this applies to: Ace the Interview Hack; The Follow-up Game; Hacks, Rituals, and Routines

Glassdoor

Glassdoor highlights employee reviews, and salaries as well as interview questions. It is an invaluable database for insight into a prospective employer. Check it out at www.Glassdoor.com

Hack this applies to: Research Companies; You Have Multiple Internship Offers, Now What?

IFTTT

IFTTT helps automate your life by creating connections between apps such as Facebook, Google Calendar, Twitter, and Gmail. Each of these automations are called "Recipes". You can install IFTTT on your smartphone to help you stay on task. Check it out at ifttt.com

Hack this applies to: Procrastination Hack

Google Drive / Dropbox

Google Drive and Dropbox are great ways to safely store your internship documents for free or at a low price. Once documents are stored in Drive or Dropbox, you will have access to them across all of your devices. Check them out at www.google.com/drive www.dropbox.com

Hacks this Applies to: Research Job Description Hack, Elevator pitch, Referral Strategy, Research Hack, The Meetup Hack

Trello

If you're looking to supercharge your to-do list, check out Trello. Trello allows you to create a board to organize a project. For example, you might create a board called "Landing an Internship" where you plan out the steps you will take toward applying for a specific internship. Trello's boards are helpful because they consist of lists and cards that you can use to prioritize and organize the necessary tasks to complete a project. Furthermore, on each card, you can add checklists to help organize subtasks. When you use hacks such as the "Research Job Description Hack", you can highlight the job descriptions that interest you on individual cards. When you get further along in the process, you can use Trello to list the top companies you want to apply to. You can also use Trello's lists for people you want to network with. With all of these capabilities, Trello is a versatile tool that could be instrumental in keeping you organized and focused while you try to land an internship. Check it out at https://trello.com/internshiphack. See a screenshot on 155.

Hacks this Applies to: all

Cold Turkey

Cold Turkey is a free productivity app available for PC and Android that temporarily blocks out online distractions. Cold Turkey helps you focus and saves you time while you do your work. The pro version allows you to block applications such as video games and also lets you set a schedule. See below. A version for Apple devices is coming out soon. Download it at getcoldturkey.com

Hacks this Applies to: Most specifically, the Procrastination hack, but this app is valuable throughout the entire process.

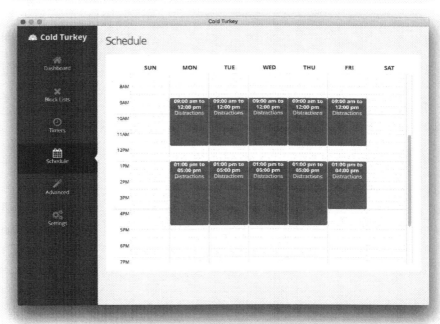

Grammarly

There is nothing worse than losing an interview or job opportunity because of your grammar! Grammarly's premium features offer integration with Microsoft Office (PC only), customized checks for professional emails, and suggestions for more effective vocabulary usage. Check it out at www.grammarly.com

Hemingway Editor

Another app to use to clean up your emails and cover letter is Hemingway Editor. It helps you simplify your writing by highlighting wordy sentences in yellow and hard to read ones in red. You also receive a grade for readability. Hemingway highlights the passages that use passive voice and messy sentence structures so you can get your message across effectively. You can also use the Hemingway app without Wi-Fi. As an added bonus, you can export your text as a Microsoft Word file.

The Hemingway Editor is available for the Mac and PC for $9.99. www.hemingwayapp.com

Personal Branding Site

about.me is a simple, one-page website that allows you to introduce yourself to employers. Rather than judging you based on just your Facebook or tweets, your about.me can show the complete story of you. With different call-to-actions, such as "Hire me," "Read my blog," or "View my portfolio," you can direct employers to what's important to you. about.me helps you control your employer's first impression of you.

Check it out at about.me/student

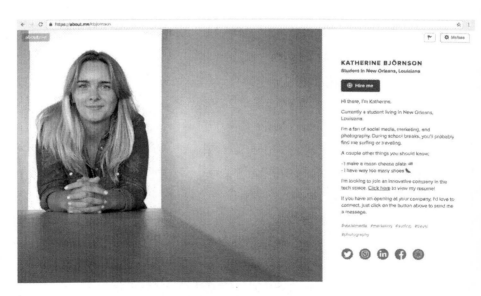

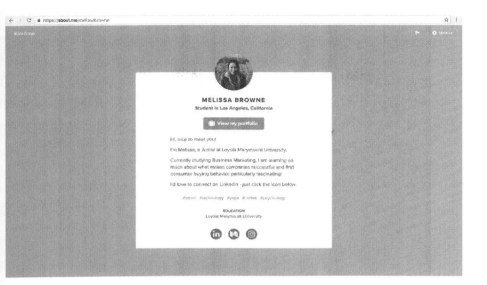

Portfolios

One easy way to impress your prospective employers is to provide them with your portfolio. A portfolio can include samples from projects you've worked on, and it can highlight your career goals. In addition to showcasing your past work and future aspirations, portfolios give prospective employers a sense of your personality. If you're unfamiliar with programming and can't code your own portfolio, you can turn to one of the many free portfolio builders online.

For example, check out Somebody.io
In under 3 minutes you can create your personal port-

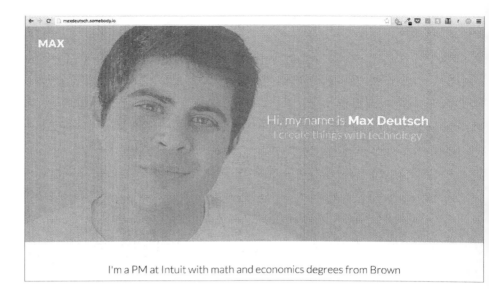

I'm a PM at Intuit with math and economics degrees from Brown

I'm a PM at Intuit with math and economics degrees from Brown

Here's my story...

In 6th grade, I sold essay-writing software to my friends in the cafeteria. I thought it used artificial intelligence, but it was basically a MadLib on a CD-ROM. Sophomore year of high school, I built a visual effects studio and my work ended up screening at the Cannes Film Festival. Senior year, I founded a biotech company (with the help of some really smart people at the NYU Langone Medical Center) to build technology that enables deaf patients to enjoy music. A lot of what we did is now clinical procedure. Sophomore year of college, I started a payments company...just so I could eat more cheaply around Brown's campus. Senior year, I launched Rhombus, a Startup-As-A-Service company, with a team of designers and engineers across eight different timezones. In 2015, I graduated, moved to SF, and started working at Intuit, building cool stuff for QuickBooks. In the meantime, I've also built portraits out of Legos, ridden thousands of miles on my bike, learned to speak Hebrew, co-founded a nationwide business publication, solved a Rubik's Cube blindfolded, started an education non-profit, published crossword puzzles in major publications, and played lots of blues guitar and jazz percussion. Then, I built Somebody.io, so anyone can build a site like this...

Check out some of my projects and passions

160

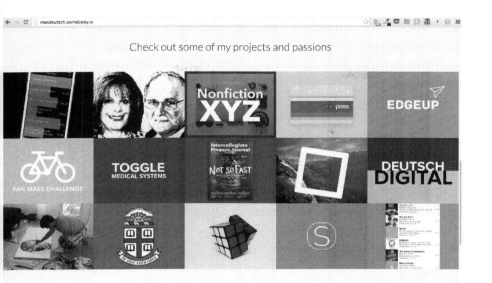

ACKNOWLEDGMENTS
BY
THE AUTHORS

I'd like to thank the many colleges and universities who have supported the work book series along our journey; our publisher, La Plata Press; my co-author Zachary; our editor, Charley; and the career services professionals whose hard work and collaboration continue to help students realize their potential.

- Bill Hobbs

I would like to thank my parents, Debbie and Charles Schleien, for all of their support. I want to thank Debby Sampayo for the countless hours you dedicated to helping me get to where I am today. I want to also thank my brother, Eric, who continuously challenges me to do everything I want in life. Lastly, I want to thank my publisher, La Plata Press; co-author, Bill; and editor, Charley for believing in me and turning this idea into a reality.

This book is a testament to my life. No one has to settle on an internship. My goal is that all students find their dream internships and in turn, their dream careers.

- Zachary Schleien

References

Burks, Stephen V., Bo Cowgill, Mitchell Hoffman, and Michael Housman, "The Value of Hiring Through Employee Referrals." *Quarterly Journal of Economics,* vol. 130, no. 2, 2015, pp. 805-839, *Business Source Premier,* doi: 10.1093/qje/qjv010. Accessed 25 Oct. 2016.

Granovetter, Mark. "The Strength of Weak Ties: A Network Theory Revisited." *Sociological Theory,* vol. 1, 1983, pp. 201-233, *Wiley,* http://www.soc.ucsb.edu/faculty/friedkin/Syllabi/Soc148/Granovetter%201983.pdf. Accessed 25 Oct. 2016.

Intern Salaries." *Salary: Intern Glassdoor,* Glassdor, 3 Nov. 2016, www.glassdoor.com/salaries/intern-salary-srch_ko0,6.htm. Accessed 9 Nov. 2016

McSpadden, Kevin. "You Now Have a Shorter Attention Span Than a Goldfish." *Time Magazine,* 14 May 2015, http://time.com/3858309/attention-spans-goldfish/. Accessed 25 Oct. 2016.

ABOUT THE AUTHORS

Bill Hobbs is an accomplished leader with a unique blend of Fortune 500, entrepreneurship, and tech startup experience who has successfully built top performing sales teams and has led large scale market expansions. He serves on the Board of Advisors for several leading software companies, and is a bestselling author. He is invited to share his experience on personal branding and career development by numerous colleges and universities. Bill is an expert in strategic change management, executive leadership, revenue strategy, organizational alignment, customer success, sales management and new market expansion.

Zachary Schleien earned a Master of Science in Information Management from the School of Information Studies at Syracuse University (Dec '15). He received his B.A. in History and a minor in Marketing ('12). He was a 2014-2015 Kauffman Entrepreneurship Engagement Fellow and has been invited by non-profits to talk on topics such as entrepreneurship and leadership. He currently works for Johnson & Johnson in their IT Leadership Development Program (ITLDP). His passions lie in growth hacking, entrepreneurship, and nutrition.

Made in the USA
Middletown, DE
08 December 2017